OTHELLO

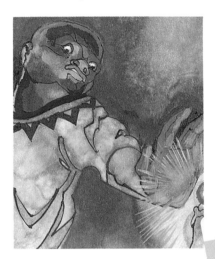

Shakespeare The Animated Tales is a multinational venture conceived by S4C,
Channel 4 Wales. Produced in Russia, Wales and England, the series has been financed by S4C
and the BBC (UK), Christmas Films (Russia), Home Box Office (USA) and Fujisankei (Japan).

Academic Panel
Professor Stanley Wells
Dr Rex Gibson

Educational Adviser
Michael Marland

Publishing Editor and Co-ordinator
Jane Fior

Book Design
Fiona Macmillan and Ness Wood

Animation Director for *Othello*
Nikolai Serebriakov of Christmas Films, Moscow

Series Editors
Martin Lamb and Penelope Middelboe, Right Angle, Tenby, Wales

Executive Producers
Christopher Grace (S4C)
Elizabeth Babakhina (Christmas Films)

Associate Producer
Theresa Plummer Andrews (BBC)

First published in 1994
by William Heinemann Ltd
an imprint of Reed Consumer Books Ltd
Michelin House, 81 Fulham Road, London SW3 6RB
and Auckland, Melbourne, Singapore and Toronto
Copyright © Shakespeare Animated Films/Christmas Films 1994

ISBN 0 434 96778 5

A CIP catalogue record for this title is available
from the British Library

Printed and bound in the UK by BPC Paulton Books Limited

The publishers would like to thank Paul Cox
for the series logo illustration,
Carol Kemp for her calligraphy,
Theo Crosby for the use of his painting of the Globe,
and Rosa Fior and Celia Salisbury Jones
for their help on the books.

Shakespeare
THE ANIMATED TALES

OTHELLO

ABRIDGED BY LEON GARFIELD

ILLUSTRATED BY NIKOLAI SEREBRIAKOV

HEINEMANN YOUNG BOOKS

William Shakespeare

WILLIAM SHAKESPEARE

NEXT TO GOD, A wise man once said, Shakespeare created most. In the thirty-seven plays that are his chief legacy to the world – and surely no-one ever left a richer! – human nature is displayed in all its astonishing variety.

He has enriched the stage with matchless comedies, tragedies, histories, and, towards the end of his life, with plays that defy all description, strange plays that haunt the imagination like visions.

His range is enormous: kings and queens, priests, princes and merchants, soldiers, clowns and drunkards, murderers, pimps, whores, fairies, monsters and pale, avenging ghosts 'strut and fret their hour upon the stage'. Murders and suicides abound; swords flash, blood flows, poison drips, and lovers sigh; yet there is always time for old men to talk of growing apples and for gardeners to discuss the weather.

In the four hundred years since they were written, they have become known and loved in every land; they are no longer the property of one country and one people, they are the priceless possession of the world.

His life, from what we know of it, was not astonishing. The stories that have attached themselves to him are remarkable only for their ordinariness: poaching deer, sleeping off a drinking bout under a wayside tree. There are no duels, no loud, passionate loves, no excesses of any kind. He was not one of your unruly geniuses whose habits are more interesting than their works. From all accounts, he was of a gentle, honourable disposition, a good businessman, and a careful father.

He was born on April 23rd 1564, to John and Mary Shakespeare of Henley Street, Stratford-upon-Avon. He was their third child and first son. When he was four or five he began his education at the local petty school. He left the local grammar school when he was about fourteen, in all probability to help in his father's glove-making shop. When he was eighteen, he married Anne Hathaway, who lived in a nearby village. By the time he was twenty-one, he was the father of three children, two daughters and a son.

Then, it seems, a restless mood came upon him. Maybe he travelled, maybe he was, as some say, a schoolmaster in the country; but at some time during the next seven years, he went to London and found employment in the theatre. When he was twenty-eight, he was already well enough known as an actor and playwright to excite the spiteful envy of a rival, who referred to him as 'an upstart crow'.

He mostly lived and worked in London until his mid-forties, when he returned to his family and home in Stratford, where he remained in prosperous circumstances until his death on April 23rd 1616, his fifty-second birthday.

He left behind him a widow, two daughters (his son died in childhood), and the richest imaginary world ever created by the human mind.

LEON GARFIELD

The list of the plays contained in the First Folio of 1623. This was the first collected edition of Shakespeare's plays and was gathered together by two of his fellow actors, John Hemmings and Henry Condell.

A CATALOGVE

of the feuerall Comedies, Hiftories, and Tragedies contained in this Volume.

THE THEATRE IN SHAKESPEARE'S DAY

IN 1989 AN ARCHAEOLOGICAL discovery was made on the south bank of the Thames that sent shivers of delight through the theatre world. A fragment of Shakespeare's own theatre, the Globe, where many of his plays were first performed, had been found.

This discovery has fuelled further interest in how Shakespeare himself conceived and staged his plays. We know a good deal already, and archaeology as well as documentary research will no doubt reveal more, but although we can only speculate on some of the details, we have a good idea of what the Elizabethan theatre-goer saw, heard and smelt when he went to see a play by William Shakespeare at the Globe.

It was an entirely different experience from anything we know today. Modern theatres have roofs to keep out the weather. If it rained on the Globe, forty per cent of the play-goers got wet. Audiences today sit on cushioned seats, and usually (especially if the play is by Shakespeare) watch and listen in respectful silence. In the Globe, the floor of the theatre was packed with a riotous crowd of garlic-reeking apprentices, house servants and artisans, who had each paid a penny to stand for the entire duration of the play, to buy nuts and apples from the food-sellers, to refresh themselves with bottled ale, relieve themselves, perhaps, into buckets by the back wall, to talk, cheer, catcall, clap and hiss if the play did not please them.

In the galleries that rose in curved tiers around the inside of the building sat those who could afford to pay two pennies for a seat, and the benefits of a roof over their heads. Here, the middle ranking citizens, the merchants, the sea captains, the clerks from the Inns of Court, would sit crammed into their small eighteen inch space and look down upon the 'groundlings' below. In the 'Lords' room', the rich and the great, noblemen and women, courtiers and foreign ambassadors had to pay sixpence each for the relative comfort and luxury of their exclusive position directly above the stage, where they smoked tobacco, and overlooked the rest.

We are used to a stage behind an arch, with wings on either side, from which the actors come on and into which they disappear. In the Globe, the stage was a platform thrusting out into the middle of the floor, and the audience, standing in the central yard, surrounded it on three sides. There were no wings. Three doors at the back of the stage were used for all exits and entrances. These were sometimes covered by a curtain, which could be used as a prop.

Today we sit in a darkened theatre or cinema, and look at a brilliantly lit stage or screen, or we sit at home in a small, private world of our own, watching a luminous television screen. The close-packed, rowdy crowd at the Globe, where the play started at two o'clock in the afternoon, had no artificial light to enhance their illusion. It was the words that moved them. They came to listen, rather than to see.

No dimming lights announced the start of the play. A blast from a trumpet and three sharp knocks warned the audience that the action was about to begin. In the broad daylight, the actor could see the audience as clearly as the audience could see him. He spoke directly to the crowd, and held them with his eyes, following their reactions. He could play up to the raucous laughter that greeted the comical, bawdy scenes, and gauge the emotional response to the higher flights of poetry. Sometimes he even improvised speeches of his own. He was surrounded by, enfolded by, his audience.

The stage itself would seem uncompromisingly bare to our eyes. There was no scenery. No painted backdrops suggested a forest, or a castle, or the sumptuous interior of a palace. Shakespeare painted the scenery with his words, and the imagination of the audience did the rest.

Props were brought onto the stage only when they were essential for the action. A bed would be carried on when a character needed to lie on it. A throne would be let down from above when a king needed to sit on it. Torches and lanterns would suggest that it was dark, but the main burden of persuading an audience, at three o'clock in the afternoon, that it was in fact the middle of the night, fell upon the language.

In our day, costume designers create a concept as part of the production of a play into which each costume fits. Shakespeare's actors were responsible for their own costumes. They would use what was to hand in the 'tiring house' (dressing room), or supplement it out of their own pockets. Classical, medieval and Tudor clothes could easily appear side by side in the same play.

No women actors appeared on a public stage until many years after

The Workes of William Shakespeare,

containing all his Comedies, Histories, and
Tragedies: Truely set forth, according to their first
O R J G J N A L L.

The Names of the Principall Actors
in all these Playes.

Illiam Shakespeare.

Richard Burbadge.

John Hemmings.

Augustine Phillips.

William Kempt.

Thomas Poope.

George Bryan.

Henry Condell.

William Slye.

Richard Cowly.

John Lowine.

Samuell Crosse.

Alexander Cooke.

Samuel Gilburne.

Robert Armin.

William Ostler.

Nathan Field.

John Underwood.

Nicholas Tooley.

William Ecclestone.

Joseph Taylor.

Robert Benfield.

Robert Goughe.

Richard Robinson.

Iohn Shancke.

Iohn Rice.

Shakespeare's death, for at that time it would have been considered shameless. The parts of young girls were played by boys. The parts of older women were played by older men.

In 1613 the Globe theatre was set on fire by a spark from a cannon during a performance of Henry VIII, and it burnt to the ground. The actors, including Shakespeare himself, dug into their own pockets and paid for it to be rebuilt. The new theatre lasted until 1642, when it closed again. Now, in the 1990s, the Globe is set to rise again as a committed band of actors, scholars and enthusiasts are raising the money to rebuild Shakespeare's theatre in its original form a few yards from its previous site.

From the time when the first Globe theatre was built until today, Shakespeare's plays have been performed in a vast variety of languages, styles, costumes and techniques, on stage, on film, on television and in animated film. Shakespeare himself, working within the round wooden walls of his theatre, would have been astonished by it all.

PATRICK SPOTTISWOODE
Director of Education,
Globe Theatre Museum

From this list of actors, we can see that William Shakespeare not only wrote plays but also acted in them. The Globe theatre, where these actors performed, is now being rebuilt close to its original site on the south bank of the river Thames.

What They Said of Him

One will ever find, in searching his works, new cause for astonishment and admiration.

GOETHE

Shakespeare was a writer of all others the most calculated to make his readers better as well as wiser.

SAMUEL TAYLOR COLERIDGE

An overstrained enthusiasm is more pardonable with respect to Shakespeare than the want of it; for our admiration cannot easily surpass his genius.

WILLIAM HAZLITT

It required three hundred years for England to begin to hear those two words that the whole world cries in her ear – William Shakespeare.

VICTOR HUGO

He has left nothing to be said about nothing or anything.

JOHN KEATS

The stream of time, which is continually washing the dissoluble fabrics of other poets, passes without injury by the adamant of Shakespeare.

SAMUEL JOHNSON

OTHELLO

This is the story of a great general, a man in whom the state of Venice has put all its trust, a black man of immense dignity and splendour who is brought to madness, murder and suicide by the skilful lies of the lieutenant he trusts and calls 'honest Iago'. "Will you, I pray," asks the tragically bewildered Othello, when Iago's villainy is discovered, "demand that demi-devil why he hath thus ensnared my soul and body?" "Demand me nothing;" answers Iago, "what you know, you know; from this time forth I never will speak word."

It is a marvellous, terrifying play, in which Shakespeare, at the very height of his powers, has created, in Iago, the most devilish villain in all drama: most devilish because, although he gives reasons for his hatred of Othello, they are too small for the monstrousness of his revenge.

THE CHARACTERS IN THE PLAY

in order of appearance

The curtain rises on a chapel. Othello the Moor, commander of all the forces of Venice, is to marry Desdemona. But it is a wedding that causes more rage than joy. Not only to Desdemona's father, Brabantio, but to Iago, Othello's ensign.

IAGO (*watching Desdemona and Othello*) I do hate him as I hate hell's pains. (*They kiss.*) O, you are well-tuned now! But I'll set down the pegs that make this music, as honest as I am.

Iago rushes through the dim and torchlit streets of Venice. He reaches Brabantio's house and bangs on the door.

IAGO Signior Brabantio, ho! Awake!

BRABANTIO What is the matter there?

IAGO Look to your house, your daughter! Even now, very now, an old black ram is tupping your white ewe! Your daughter and the Moor are now making the beast with two backs!

Brabantio searches his house and discovers his daughter gone. With armed servants, he rushes through the streets to Othello's lodging and thunders on the door.

BRABANTIO Who would be a father?

OTHELLO Keep up your bright swords for the dew will rust them!

BRABANTIO O thou foul thief! Where hast thou stowed my daughter?

OTHELLO Where will you that I go and answer to this charge?

In the council chamber, Brabantio throws himself before the duke and accuses Othello who stands by with Iago.

BRABANTIO   Oh, my daughter is abused, stolen from me and corrupted by witchcraft and medicines!

DUKE   (*to Othello*) What can you say to this?

OTHELLO   That I have ta'en away this old man's daughter, it is most true. True I have married her. This only is the witchcraft I have used . . . Her father loved me, oft invited me, still questioned me the story of my life. She loved me for the dangers I had passed, and I loved her, that she did pity them.

The duke and his fellow dignitaries listen entranced to Othello's adventures.

DUKE   I think this tale would win my daughter too. Valiant Othello, we must straight employ you against the general enemy. You must hence tonight.

At the crowded quayside, Venetian ships make ready to set sail for Cyprus. Brabantio shouts to Othello who is already aboard.

BRABANTIO   Look to her, Moor, if thou hast eyes to see: she has deceived her father and may thee! (*He points to another ship on which Desdemona stands.*)

OTHELLO   My life upon her faith!

He waves to Desdemona, who waves back, with a strawberry-spotted handkerchief. Iago watches Othello and salutes him. Othello cordially returns the gesture. Roderigo, an elegant young gallant, sidles up beside Iago, gazing in a love-sick way at Desdemona.

IAGO   (*nudging Roderigo suggestively*) I have told thee often, I hate the Moor. If thou canst cuckold him, thou dost thyself a pleasure, and me a sport.

Roderigo smiles hopefully, and slips some money into Iago's ready hand. He departs.

The fleet sets sail but a storm springs up and before long drives the vessels apart. The first ship to reach Cyprus carries Cassio, a young man Othello has promoted over Iago's head to be his lieutenant; then comes a vessel carrying Iago and his wife Emilia, lady-in-waiting to Othello's bride.

CASSIO   (*greeting Desdemona as she disembarks*) O behold, the riches of the ship is come ashore! Hail to thee, lady!

He kneels and kisses his fingers in gallant admiration of Desdemona. She extends her hand, which Cassio takes fondly, and rises, kissing her hand as he does so.

IAGO   (*aside*) Very good, well kissed, an excellent courtesy. With as little a web as this will I ensnare as great a fly as Cassio.

DESDEMONA   What tidings can you tell me of my lord?

CASSIO   He is not yet —

He is interrupted by a cry of 'A sail, A sail!' Desdemona looks eagerly to sea. Cassio kisses Emilia.

IAGO   Sir, would she give you so much of her lips as of her tongue she oft bestows on me, you'd have enough.

DESDEMONA   Alas, she has no speech!

CASSIO   Lo, where he comes.

Othello appears and greets Desdemona.

OTHELLO O, my fair warrior!

DESDEMONA My dear Othello!

They embrace, as Iago looks on. Then all depart, except for Iago and Roderigo. Iago beckons to Roderigo who draws close.

IAGO Lieutenant Cassio tonight watches on the court of guard. First, I must tell thee this: Desdemona is directly in love with him.

RODERIGO I cannot believe that in her; she's full of most blest condition!

IAGO Blest pudding! Didst thou not see her paddle with the palm of his hand?

RODERIGO Well?

IAGO Do you find some occasion to anger Cassio. He's rash, and haply may strike at you. So shall you have a shorter journey to your desires . . .

It is night. In a courtyard, Cassio and a group of officers are seated round a table on which there are bottles of wine. Iago enters.

CASSIO   Welcome, Iago; we must to the watch.

IAGO   Not this hour, lieutenant; I have a stoup of wine –

He produces a bottle, and offers it to Cassio.

CASSIO   Not tonight, good Iago; I have very poor and unhappy brains for drinking.

IAGO   But one cup – (*Cassio protests and turns away. The others try to tempt him.*) If I can fasten but one cup upon him, he'll be as full of quarrel and offence as my young mistress' dog. (*Iago sees that Cassio still resists and approaches him, the bottle in hand.*) Some wine, ho! (*He seizes hold of Cassio affectionately. Music strikes up. Iago sings.*)

> And let me the cannikin clink, clink.
> And let me the cannikin clink;
> A soldier's a man,
> O, man's life's but a span,
> Why then, let a soldier drink!
> Why then, let a soldier drink!

Some wine . . . Cassio!

During the song, Iago begins to whirl Cassio round and round, laughingly forcing wine down his throat. The others join in. The dance becomes wild and whirling. At the height of it, Roderigo appears and taunts Cassio. Madly, drunkenly, Cassio draws his sword.

CASSIO   Villain! Villain, knave!

Roderigo flees. Officers try to restrain Cassio, but he is incensed. He fights and wounds Montano. In the midst of the uproar, Othello enters.

OTHELLO   Hold for your lives! What is the matter, masters? Who began this? (*They all fall back, and leave the wretched, drunken Cassio swaying, with his bloody sword in his hand. Othello looks at him sorrowfully.*) Cassio, I love thee, but never more be officer of mine.

All depart. Cassio is left alone, weeping with shame. Iago insinuates himself beside him.

IAGO   What, are you hurt, lieutenant?

CASSIO   Ay, past all surgery. O, I have lost the immortal part of myself. My reputation, Iago, my reputation!

IAGO   As I am an honest man, I thought you had received some bodily wound.

CASSIO   Drunk! And speak like a parrot! O God.

IAGO   Come, come, I'll tell you what you shall do. Our general's wife is now the general. Confess yourself freely to her, importune her – she'll help to put you in your place again.

CASSIO   You advise me well. I will beseech the virtuous Desdemona to undertake for me. Good night, honest Iago.

Iago smiles after him.

IAGO   For whiles this honest fool plies Desdemona to repair his fortunes, and she for him pleads strongly to the Moor, I'll pour this pestilence into his ear: that she repeals him for her body's lust. So will I turn her virtue into pitch, and out of her own goodness make the net that shall enmesh them all!

Next morning, Cassio takes Iago's advice. He approaches Desdemona in the palace garden and begs her to plead his cause with Othello.

DESDEMONA   Be thou assured, good Cassio, I will do all my abilities in thy behalf. (*Cassio, ever the gentleman, fervently kisses her hand. She laughs.*) Therefore be merry, Cassio –

EMILIA   Madam, here comes my lord!

CASSIO   (*hastily*) Madam, I'll take my leave.

He hastens away as Othello appears, accompanied by Iago. Iago glares at the retreating Cassio.

IAGO   Ha! I like not that.

OTHELLO   What dost thou say?

IAGO   Nothing my lord.

OTHELLO   Was not that Cassio that parted from my wife?

IAGO   Cassio, my lord? No, sure I cannot think it, that he would steal away so guilty-like, seeing you coming.

OTHELLO   I do believe 'twas he. Is he not honest?

IAGO   My lord, for aught I know.

Othello stares at Iago, who shakes his head, looking at Desdemona.

OTHELLO   I think so too.

IAGO   Why, then I think Cassio's an honest man.

OTHELLO   I know thou art full of honesty, and weigh'st thy words. Thou dost mean something . . .

IAGO   Oh, beware jealousy, my lord! It is the green-eyed monster.

OTHELLO	Farewell, if more thou dost perceive, let me know more. (*Iago leaves. Othello gazes towards Desdemona.*) Excellent wretch! Perdition catch my soul but I do love thee; and when I love thee not, chaos is come again!
DESDEMONA	Good love, call him back.
OTHELLO	Who is't you mean?
DESDEMONA	Why, your lieutenant, Cassio.
OTHELLO	Not now, sweet Desdemona, some other time.
DESDEMONA	Shall't be tonight at supper?
OTHELLO	No, not tonight.
DESDEMONA	Why then, tomorrow night –
OTHELLO	I do beseech thee, to leave me but a little by myself.
DESDEMONA	Are you not well?
OTHELLO	I have a pain upon my forehead here.

DESDEMONA   Let me but bind your head, within this hour it will be well again.

OTHELLO   Your napkin is too little. (*He pushes the handkerchief aside and she drops it.*) Let it alone.

Emilia, left behind, picks up the handkerchief.

EMILIA   This was her first remembrance from the Moor. My wayward husband hath a hundred times wooed me to steal it; but she so loves the token —

Iago enters.

IAGO   What do you here alone?

EMILIA   I have a thing for you. What will you give me now for that same handkerchief?

IAGO   A good wench! Give it to me. (*He snatches it.*) I will in Cassio's lodging lose this napkin and let him find it. Trifles light as air are to the jealous confirmations strong as proofs of holy writ. This may do something. The Moor already changes with my poison . . .

As he speaks, Othello approaches. His countenance is tormented as his fearful thoughts present him, over and over again, with the vision of Cassio kissing his wife's hand, until the kiss becomes lascivious.

IAGO   Look where he comes! Not poppy nor mandragora, nor all the drowsy syrups of the world, shall ever medicine thee to that sweet sleep which thou owed'st yesterday.

OTHELLO   (*seizing Iago by the throat*) Villain, be sure thou prove my love a whore! Or woe upon thy life!

IAGO   (*freeing himself*) O grace! O heaven defend me! Take note, take note, O world! To be direct and honest is not safe.

He retreats.

OTHELLO   Nay, stay; give me a living reason, that she's disloyal.

IAGO   I do not like the office; but I will go on. I lay with Cassio lately. In sleep, I heard him say, 'Sweet Desdemona, let us be wary, let us hide our loves'.

OTHELLO   O monstrous, monstrous!

IAGO   Nay, this was but his dream –

OTHELLO   I'll tear her all to pieces!

IAGO   Nay, yet be wise; she may be honest yet. Have you not seen a handkerchief spotted with strawberries in your wife's hand?

OTHELLO   I gave her such a one; 'twas my first gift.

IAGO   I know not that; but such a handkerchief – I am sure it was your wife's – did I today see Cassio wipe his beard with.

OTHELLO   O blood, Iago, blood! Within these three days let me hear thee say that Cassio's not alive.

IAGO   My friend is dead: 'tis done as you request. But let her live.

OTHELLO   Damn her, lewd minx! Come, go with me apart. Now art thou my lieutenant.

IAGO   I am your own for ever.

In another part of the garden, Desdemona searches for the lost handkerchief. Emilia is with her.

DESDEMONA   Where should I lose that handkerchief, Emilia?

EMILIA   I know not, madam.

Othello enters.

DESDEMONA   How is't with you, my lord?

OTHELLO   I have a salt and sorry rheum offends me; lend me thy handkerchief.

DESDEMONA   Here, my lord.

OTHELLO   That which I gave you.

DESDEMONA   I have it not about me.

OTHELLO   That's a fault. That handkerchief did an Egyptian to my mother give. She told her, while she kept it, 'twould subdue my father entirely to her love; but if she lost it or made a gift of it, my father's eye should hold her loathly . . .

DESDEMONA   Then would to God that I had never seen't!

OTHELLO   Is't lost? Is't gone?

DESDEMONA	Heaven bless us! This is a trick to put me from my suit. Pray you let Cassio be received again.
OTHELLO	Fetch me that handkerchief.
DESDEMONA	I pray, talk me of Cassio.
OTHELLO	The handkerchief!

He rushes away like a madman. But the handkerchief has gone. Iago has put it in Cassio's lodging and Cassio, finding it and liking it, has given it to Bianca, his mistress, to copy.

Still searching for the handkerchief, Desdemona and Emilia leave the garden and presently Iago and Othello enter together. Othello leans almost pathetically, towards his new lieutenant. He is sweating and seems unwell.

OTHELLO	What hath he said?
IAGO	Faith, that he did – I know not what he did.
OTHELLO	But, what?
IAGO	Lie –

OTHELLO   With her?

IAGO   With her, on her, what you will.

OTHELLO   Lie with her? Lie on her? Handkerchief – confessions –
           handkerchief! Is't possible? O devil!

*During the above wild outburst. Othello is overwhelmed by
hateful fancies, which finally dissolve into a red oblivion, like
the fires of hell. Gradually the fragmented images solidify into
Iago's face, looking down, much concerned.*

IAGO   How is it, general? Whilst you were here, mad with your grief,
           Cassio came hither. I shifted him away; bade him anon return
           and here speak with me. Do but encave yourself, for I will
           make him tell the tale anew, where, how, how oft, how long
           ago, and when he has and is again to cope your wife. Will you
           withdraw?

*Othello, helplessly in the power of Iago, nods and hides
himself behind a trellis, like a netted beast. Cassio approaches.*

IAGO   (*to himself*) Now will I question Cassio of Bianca. As he shall
           smile, Othello shall go mad.

Iago, with the skill of a dancer, leads Cassio, whispering in his ear, close to the trellis behind which Othello listens.

IAGO   (*to Cassio, aloud*) I never knew a woman love man so.

CASSIO   (*laughing*) Alas, poor rogue! I think i' faith she loves me. She hangs and lolls and weeps upon me, so hales and pulls me . . .

OTHELLO   Now he tells how she plucked him to my chamber. O, I see that nose of yours, but not the dog I shall throw it to!

Bianca enters. She is clutching the handkerchief.

BIANCA   (*flourishing it*) This is some minx's token, and I must take out the work? There!

OTHELLO   By heaven, that should be my handkerchief!

Bianca throws the handkerchief at Cassio, and stalks away indignantly.

IAGO   After her, after her!

CASSIO   Faith, I must. She'll rail in the streets else. (*He follows.*)

OTHELLO   (*emerging from concealment*) How shall I murder him, Iago? I would have him nine years a-killing. A fine woman, a fair woman, a sweet woman!

IAGO   Nay, you must forget that.

OTHELLO   No, my heart is turned to stone. I strike it, and it hurts my
            hand. O, the world hath not a sweeter creature! O Iago, the
            pity of it, Iago!

IAGO   If you are so fond over her iniquity –

OTHELLO   Get me some poison, Iago, this night. This night, Iago!

IAGO   Do it not with poison; strangle her in her bed, even the bed she
            hath contaminated. And for Cassio, let me be his undertaker.

OTHELLO   Good, good! The justice of it pleases.

*A trumpet sounds. The two men stare. At the harbour,
Lodovico, the ambassador from the duke, disembarks and is
greeted by Desdemona. Othello, accompanied by Iago,
appears and Lodovico gives him a letter.*

LODOVICO   (*to Othello*) The Duke and Senators of Venice greet you.
            (*To Desdemona*) How does Lieutenant Cassio?

            Frowning, Othello moves away, reading.

DESDEMONA   Cousin, there's fallen between him and my lord an unkind
            breach; I would do much to atone them, for the love I bear to
            Cassio.

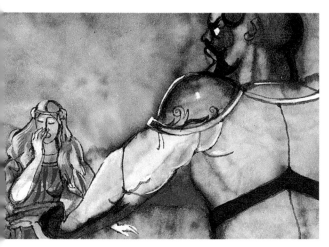 

OTHELLO   Devil! (*He strikes her.*)

DESDEMONA   (*weeping*) I have not deserved this.

LODOVICO   (*comforting her*) Maybe the letter moved him for as I think they do command him home. (*To Othello*) My lord, make her amends; she weeps.

OTHELLO   O devil, devil! Out of my sight! (*Bewildered, Desdemona departs.*) Sir, I obey the mandate, and will return to Venice.

Othello rushes away.

LODOVICO   (*to Iago*) Is this the noble Moor whom our full senate call all-in-all sufficient? Are his wits safe?

IAGO   Alas, alas! It is not honesty in me to speak what I have seen and known. Do but go after and mark how he continues . . .

Desdemona's bedchamber. She is seated with Emilia. Othello enters.

OTHELLO   Let me see your eyes; look in my face. (*He dismisses Emilia with a wave of his hand. She goes.*) What art thou?

DESDEMONA   Your wife, my lord, your true and loyal wife.

OTHELLO   Are you not a strumpet?

DESDEMONA   No, as I shall be saved!

OTHELLO   I cry you mercy. I took you for that cunning whore of Venice that married with Othello.

He rushes from the room. Emilia returns with Iago, to comfort Desdemona.

EMILA   How do you, madam?

IAGO   What is the matter, my lady?

EMILIA   He called her whore.

DESDEMONA   O good Iago, what shall I do to win my lord again?

IAGO   'Tis but his humour, the business of the state does him offence, and he does chide with you. Weep not, all things shall be well. (*He leaves.*)

DESDEMONA   (*as Emilia unpins her hair and begins to brush it.*) How foolish are our minds! My mother had a maid called Barbary, and he she loved proved mad, and did forsake her; she had a song of 'willow', and she died singing it; that song tonight will not go from my mind.

EMILIA   Come, come, you talk.

DESDEMONA   (*singing*)
> The poor soul sat sighing by a sycamore tree,
> Sing all a green willow;
> Her hand on her bosom, her head on her knee,
> Sing willow, willow, willow,
> Sing willow, willow, willow,
> Must be my garland . . .

As she sings, Othello, by an open window, hears the song faintly. He frowns and stares down into the dark town below. There, Iago waits in the street near the palace for Roderigo.

IAGO   If thou hast purpose, courage, valour, then this night show it.

RODERIGO   I have no great devotion to the deed . . .

IAGO   Fear nothing, I'll be at thy elbow.

Cassio bids farewell to Bianca and comes out into the street.

IAGO   (*to himself*) Whether he kill Cassio, or Cassio him, or each do kill the other, every way makes my game.

A scuffle of shadows. Roderigo attacks Cassio. He falls and is himself wounded. He crawls away. Iago darts forward and stabs Cassio from behind, and then vanishes into concealment. There are shouts and cries.

CASSIO Help, ho! Murder, murder!

Othello, still by the window, hears the shout.

OTHELLO The voice of Cassio: Iago keeps his word. O brave Iago, thou hast such noble sense of thy friend's wrong! Thou teachest me . . . (*He leaves the room.*)

The street is alive with torches and anxious faces, surrounding the wounded Cassio. Among them are Lodovico and Iago.

IAGO   O my lieutenant! What villains have done this?

A voice calls from the shadows.

RODERIGO'S VOICE   O, help me here!

CASSIO   That's one of them!

IAGO   (*finding Roderigo*) O murderous slave! (*He stabs him.*)

RODERIGO   O damned Iago! O inhuman dog! (*He dies.*)

IAGO   (*staring up towards the castle from which Othello has looked down*) This is the night that either makes me, or fordoes me quite.

In her bedchamber, Desdemona lies on her bed. She closes her eyes. Quietly, Othello enters. He gazes first at the sleeping Desdemona, then at the candle beside her.

OTHELLO	Put out the light, and then put out the light: if I quench thee, thou flaming minister, I can again thy former light restore, should I repent me; but once put out thy light – (*He frowns, then bends to kiss her.*)
DESDEMONA	Othello?
OTHELLO	Ay, Desdemona.
DESDEMONA	Will you come to bed, my lord?
OTHELLO	Have you prayed tonight, Desdemona?
DESDEMONA	Ay, my lord.
OTHELLO	If you bethink yourself of any crime unreconciled as yet to heaven and grace, solicit for it straight. I would not kill thy unprepared spirit.
DESDEMONA	Then heaven have mercy on me!
OTHELLO	The handkerchief which I so loved, and gave thee, thou gavest to Cassio.
DESDEMONA	I never gave it him, send for him hither –

OTHELLO	He has confessed.
DESDEMONA	What, my lord?
OTHELLO	That he hath . . . used thee.
DESDEMONA	He will not say so!
OTHELLO	No, his mouth is stopped.
DESDEMONA	Alas, he is betrayed, and I undone!

Othello seizes a pillow.

OTHELLO	Down, strumpet!
DESDEMONA	Kill me tomorrow, let me live tonight!
OTHELLO	Nay, an' you strive –
DESDEMONA	But half an hour!
OTHELLO	It is too late!

He presses the pillow down on her face to suffocate her. There is a knocking on the door.

EMILIA'S VOICE	My lord, my lord!
OTHELLO	'Tis Emilia! If she come in, she'll sure speak to my wife – my wife, my wife! What wife? I have no wife! O insupportable –
EMILIA	I do beseech you that I may speak with you!
OTHELLO	O, come in, Emilia.

He draws the bed curtains and goes to unlock the door. Emilia enters and moves towards the bed.

DESDEMONA	(*faintly*) O falsely, falsely murdered!
EMILIA	(*rushing to draw back the bed curtains*) O, lady, speak again! Who hath done this deed?
DESDEMONA	Nobody; I myself. Commend me to my kind lord. O farewell. (*She dies.*)
OTHELLO	She's like a liar gone to burning hell: 'twas I that killed her!
EMILIA	O, the more angel she, and you the blacker devil!
OTHELLO	She was as false as water!
EMILIA	Thou as rash as fire to say that she was false!
OTHELLO	Cassio did top her: ask thy husband else.
EMILIA	My husband?
OTHELLO	Ay, 'twas he that told me first –
EMILIA	My husband?
OTHELLO	I say thy husband. My friend, thy husband, honest, honest Iago.
EMILIA	If he say so, may his pernicious soul rot half a grain a day! Help, help, ho! help! The Moor hath killed my mistress!

Montano and Iago burst into the room. They see the murdered Desdemona.

MONTANO   O monstrous act!

OTHELLO   'Tis pitiful; but yet Iago knows that she with Cassio hath the act of shame a thousand times committed. Cassio confessed it, and she did gratify his amorous works with the recognisance and pledge of love which I first gave her. I saw it in his hand: it was a handkerchief.

EMILIA   'Twill out, it will out! O thou dull Moor, that handkerchief thou speakest on I found by fortune and did give my husband. He begged of me to steal it –

IAGO   Filth, thou liest!

He stabs Emilia from behind, and escapes. Emilia falls, dying, on the bed. Montano pursues Iago.

EMILIA   (*dying*) Moor, she was chaste; she loved thee, cruel Moor.

She dies. Othello gazes down upon the dead Desdemona. With horror he begins to understand the full extent of Iago's treachery.

OTHELLO   O ill-starred wench! Pale as thy smock! When we shall meet at compt this look of thine will hurl my soul from heaven and fiends will snatch at it. Cold, cold my girl, even like thy chastity.

Montano, Lodovico, and the wounded Cassio enter with Iago, guarded. Othello stares at Iago, and approaches him.

OTHELLO   If that thou be'st a devil, I cannot kill thee. (*He wounds him with his sword. At once, soldiers disarm him.*)

IAGO   I bleed, sir, but not killed.

LODOVICO   This wretch hath part confessed his villainy.

CASSIO   Dear general, I did never give you cause.

OTHELLO   I do believe it, and I ask your pardon. Will you, I pray, demand that demi-devil why he hath thus ensnared my soul and body?

IAGO   Demand me nothing; what you know, you know. From this time forth I never will speak word.

LODOVICO   (*to Othello*) You must forsake this room and go with us —

OTHELLO   Soft you, a word or two. I have done the state some service and they know't. I pray you in your letters when you shall these unlucky deeds relate, speak of them as they are; nothing extenuate nor set down aught in malice. Then must you speak of one that loved not wisely, but too well. Set you down this; and say besides that in Aleppo once where a malignant and a turbaned Turk beat a Venetian and traduced the state, I took by the throat the circumcised dog and smote him thus! (*He stabs himself and falls beside Desdemona.*) I kissed thee ere I killed thee: no way but this, killing myself, to die upon a kiss.

The curtain falls.

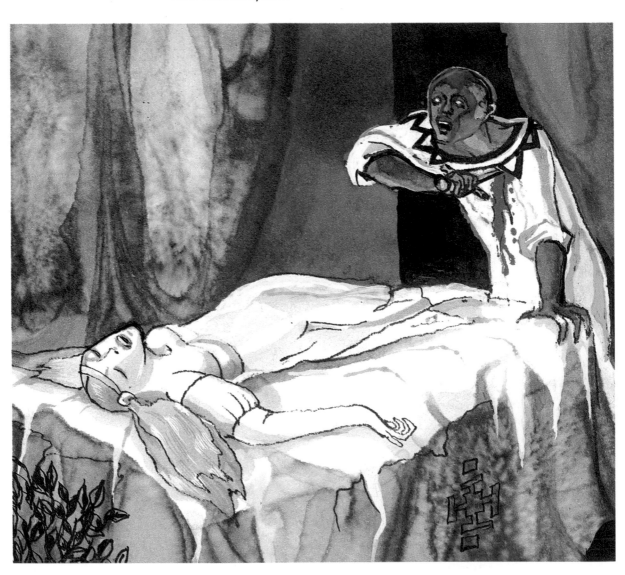